WHAT THE 99% SHOULD KNOW
(and the 1% ain't saying)

A manifesto written by a member of the 99%

By Anonymous

Book cover design by Rodney Burlingame

"All tyranny needs to gain a foothold is for people of good conscience to remain silent."

— Thomas Jefferson
3rd President of the United States
1743-1826

Dedicated to the honorable men, women and families of the
United States Armed Forces

To Summer
Thanks for believing in me

Table of Contents

Opening

"They don't want an educated population capable of critical thinking. They don't want people who can sit around a kitchen table and figure out how badly they're getting f--ked by a system that threw them overboard 30 f---ing years ago. What they want are obedient workers. People who are just smart enough to run the machines and do the paperwork, but are dumb enough to accept increasingly shi--ier jobs, the longer hours, the lower pay, the reduced benefits, the end of overtime, and the vanishing pension that disappears the moment you go to collect it. And now they're coming for your Social Security money. They want you to give it back so they can give it to their criminal friends on Wall Street."

George Carlin, American Comedian
1937-2008

Watch this prophetic George Carlin comedy routine on You Tube:
http://www.youtube.com/watch?v=T0CjAjrSieI

Introduction

I don't like to camp. But being a supportive spectator of the Occupy Wall Street Movement has preoccupied me over the past few months. People say it's a misguided protest. I don't agree. It may be a little unorganized, but the OWS protesters do have a valid point.

It's important that someone is pointing a finger, because a catastrophic event has taken place in the U.S. economy, even though the devastation has not been properly or accurately articulated by the press, the pundits, the professors, the analysts, the radio show hosts or the politicians. They can't wrap their heads around the economic sinkhole we're in because they're not living in it. That's because they're members of the 1%.

The 1% talking to the 1%. All we've seen over the last few years of Sunday morning news shows, hearings, speeches and debates is the 1% talking with the 1%. The voice of the 99% has been eliminated from the discourse, because we're speechless, dealing with the shock of our new poverty. We see one billionaire talk show host talking to a generously paid expert about how to roll over your 401k in "times like these." What the 1% don't understand is our 401ks are long gone. Our homes are gone. Our jobs are gone. We have no health care coverage. We can't afford to send our kids to college. We can't afford to pay the heating bill or fill our gas tanks. We can't even afford to get our teeth cleaned.

You have to give the Occupy Wall Streeters some credit.
They have had the guts to say to the world, *"Hey, things are not fine."* Yet the pundits, news show hosts and members of the 1% keep undermining OWS, questioning who the Occupy Wall Street movement is (a bunch of crazy heroin addicts?) and casting doubt upon the overall OWS message. The mayors are going after them. The politicians can't wait to get rid of them because OWS is shedding light on the U.S.'s most serious problem: newly poor Americans and even *poorer* poor Americans. Occupy Wall Street is making noise about the dominance of Wall Street, the mega wealth of the 1% and the explosion of Lobbyist's power. It's time someone did.

Occupy Wall Street has the right idea but their method is impractical. Most of us can't go on an unending camping trip. We have kids, four jobs, lawns to mow, bills we're struggling to pay, you name it. We're busy trying to survive.

But we can still put our protests in the mail.
This may sound old fashioned and some will say it's naive, but we can fill mailrooms with our outrage. Not just any mailrooms. The mailrooms of Congress. The mailrooms of major U.S. corporations who are squirreling their way out of paying taxes. We can fill mailrooms until they're about to burst. We can mail our protest to Congress that Wall Street thugs should do hard jail time. We can mail our insistence that paid corporate lobbyists are out of control. We can insist that our Social Security and Medicare remain untouched. Good old U.S. mail. More on that later.

We can regain our power. The 99% can no longer pretend that "everything will be all right." We now know that the majority of the current members of Congress don't operate on our behalf. We know that Washington paid corporate lobbyists are running the show. We've been blindsided and gutted, deceived and stabbed in the back. But we are not powerless. And we can change things because we're still more powerful that the 1% because *we are the 99%*.

Chapter 1: A Forgotten People

I hold in my hand a 10/29/11 graph compiled by Bertelsmann Stiffung entitled *"Social Justice in the OECD – How do the Member States Compare?"* The graph lists the countries who are truly serving their citizenship and which countries aren't. Guess where the United States places on the list? We're in the bottom five, *along with Mexico.* Go ahead, Google it. You'll find that even *Slovakia* provides more support for their population than the United States does.

Here's the link:
http://www.nytimes.com/2011/10/29/opinion/blow-americas-exploding-pipe-dream.html

Congress doesn't think this is a problem. From the windows of their SUV limos, they don't see how deeply unraveled the interior of the U.S. has become. From their gated communities and insulated neighborhoods of McMansions, they can't see families getting thrown out of their houses. From the windows of their Gulf Streams, they set their sights on Afghanistan, not the ravages of downtown Detroit. This is true of *all* the members of political parties: Republicans, Democrats, Libertarians, the Tea Party, the whole stinkin' lot have big plans and agendas that don't include the 99%.

I have a better shot at gaining financial assistance from *The Ellen Degeneres Show* than an American elected official or governmental body. The Congress has ceased helping the 99%. American citizens have become invisible. We have been forgotten.

Last year, the United States gave away $39.4 billion dollars in Foreign Aid. And yet, politicians have the gall to denounce the runaway U.S. debt and point to our Medicare and our Social Security as debt-relief sources. *No way.* They aren't touching *my* Social Security. And that should be your attitude, too.

Politicians have driven us into this ditch. Fact is, we're in a national financial crisis because *Congress overspends, benefiting* other countries. Above all, we put these pols at the wheel. So we're all to blame.

Self Loyalty over Party Loyalty. We, as the 99%, must stop being immobilized over our party loyalties and support only the most effective candidates. Preferably, candidates who are not members of the 1%. We have to stop battling over conservatism versus liberalism. It's a waste of breath.

Instead, let's question the bi-partisan *global tack* American politicians have taken. Because when you think about it, *has global been all that great for the 99%?* No. If you look at Europe right now, going global wasn't a good decision at all. Going global has *helped bring the 99% down.* We've been footing the bill as Congress has been financially supporting the world and helping everyone *except us.*

"When the North American Free Trade Agreement was first signed in 1994, proponents said it would eventually create jobs for the U.S. economy. 17 years later, a new report estimates, the American worker only has hundreds of thousands of job losses to show for it. According to a report by Economic Policy Institute economist Robert Scott, entitled "Heading South: U.S.-Mexico trade and job displacement after NAFTA," an estimated 682,900 U.S. jobs have been "lost or displaced" because of the agreement and the resulting trade deficit." — *The Huffington Post,* 5/12/11

America is a great country. It's also a young, willful country. When you travel to Britain, France, Italy, Spain, you realize how *old* those countries are. You also realize that at one point, each of these countries was a dominant world leader, and today, they're not. There's a reason for that.

Older, wiser countries stopped being World Boss for one big reason: it's expensive. It's also unrealistic. The U.S. is in deep, internal trouble, and nobody knows it better than the 99%. We wonder why U.S. foreign policy makers continue to financially support other countries when *it's the American people who need rescuing.*

Wade through this quote (it's worth it):
"Economically, globalization has led to a period of prosperity around the world. It brought about industrialization at unprecedented speed and scale in developing countries of which China is the most notable one. In developed countries, dramatic economic benefits have been realized from technological advances and increased efficiency in capital allocation. This process has been undertaken within a global economic and security infrastructure led and underwritten by the U.S. A myriad of global organizations such as the WTO, the IMF, and the World Bank provide the institutional framework within which goods and capital flow ever more freely. The physical sea lanes vital to it all are kept open and safe by the U.S. Navy. American political and military power safeguard the delicate balance of the Middle East -- the source of energy for this global industrial expansion. The complex web of U.S. built security alliances around the globe has kept the world from any major destructive military conflicts. All these global "public goods" are provided by the U.S. part and parcel to its ownership of the century." – *Eric X. Li, Chairman, Chunqiu Institute, Huffington Post 12/6/11*

It's nice that we're so generous. And while it's nice that the United States will go down in our own history books as "owning" the last century, it's been at the cost of the 99%. While I feel bad for people in disadvantaged countries, I feel worse for my own kid who — since 9/11 — has watched the 99% sliding down the tubes. While Senators fly off on fact-finding missions, the United States gave $4,102,000,000.00 in foreign aid to Afghanistan in 2010. Yet this year they're reducing the number of Pell Grants to U.S. college students. Where is the honor in that? They're cutting fuel assistance to the poor and the elderly. Is that honorable? They're taxing Social Security and Unemployment benefits. *Any kindergartener will tell you, that's not fair!*

We're overly generous. It appears that the priorities of our elected politicians – *and I'm not going to call them public servants, because they're not serving the public ---* are largely set on everything and everybody outside of the United States.

"If our Founding Fathers wanted us to care about the rest of the world, they wouldn't have declared their independence from it."

—Stephen Colbert
Comedian, Writer & Actor

We have to turn our elected official's sights inward, to repair a fundamentally flawed system that overly rewards (a) Wall Street, (b) the politically powerful, (c) other countries and (d) turns a blind eye to the crafty machinations of 1%. We have to bring the focus back to the 99%.

Class warfare is already being waged. Recently, politicians were tossing around the phrase, "class warfare." Class warfare doesn't have anything to do with that misguided Wisconsin Representative's assessment that taxing the rich would result in class warfare. What politicians and the 1% don't understand is----- *class warfare is already here.*

It's the Haves vs. The Used-To-Haves.
The former members of the Middle Class have lost their health insurance, homes and vacations. Our kids can't afford college. We can't even get credit to buy a used car. We can't afford to retire, *ever*. We have been treading water since 9/11, operating on the premise that "things will get better eventually." We've been draining our 401ks, burning through our savings, going from homeowners to renters, and generally watching our foothold slide beneath our scampering feet. Our credit ratings stink. Nobody will lend to us. And now, it's clear: *things are not going to get better unless we do something to help ourselves.*

The Used-To-Haves will prevail. I am a Used-To-Have. And we're different than the Never Hads. We're angrier. We're enraged. We've had our lives ripped up. We've had a taste of being Middle Class and we haven't forgotten what we've lost. So instead of feeling powerless and forgotten, we have to get really, really worked up. We have to kick some butt. We have to get some attention! What's important now is to become determined to regain what we used to have. And maybe we'll help some of the Never Hads along the way.

Here's how change begins: It's very old fashioned. But it's effective. You may not believe me, but if we all do this, it will work.
- Begin to write letters. Not long letters – really short and clear letters, explaining how things must change.
- Mail your letters to the addresses I've included in this book.

- I know what you're thinking. You're thinking, "but I write and email and call my representatives all the time and nothing changes." That's because you're communicating to their individual offices. When you contact your lawmaker via their office, they can bury your phone call or email. Emails and phone calls have no visible presence. They're invisible, so it's like you never attempted contact.
- But if you *mail a letter* to the *overall address* of a task force or a Senate committee, with the routing info on the bottom, such as, "Attention: Senator Scott Brown" along the bottom, that piece of mail goes to the main mailroom. Don't put a detailed return address on the outside envelope. Just something like, "Jane Doe, Cleveland, OH." When a mailroom fills up with written demands from the American voters, they got a crisis on their hands. And crisis gets attention.
- Here's your first address to write to:

The U.S. Capitol Building
House of Representatives
Washington DC 20515
[EXAMPLE] Att: Rep. Don Young, Alaska

Inside, your letter should be short and concise. Say for example, if you were really writing to Rep. Don Young of Alaska, you'd say something like,
"Dear Don,
You'd better start showing up for House votes. Because I'm working on legislation that terminates your pay and benefits when you don't show up for work.
Sincerely,
Jane Doe
Cleveland, OH"

Let's fill up the main mailrooms of Congress. Further in the book, you'll see I've included individual committee addresses of all of these useless congressional committees. Yes, you can still waste your time by contacting your representative's individual office via mail, email or phone.

Just visit www.house.gov or **www.senate.gov** for the individual contact information. But trust me, your communication will get buried. Oh, you may get a form letter from your representative thanking you. But you won't get action. That's why I recommend filling mailrooms with mail demanding attention from the 1%. When you fill up a mailroom, you get attention. It's not as dramatic as camping out in a financial district, but hey, you and I have other stuff to do.

"If you need a helping hand, you can find one at the end of your arm."

—Katharine Hepburn
Academy Award Winning American Actress
1907-2003

Chapter 2: The U.S. Congress

"Reader, suppose you were an idiot. And suppose you were a member of Congress. But I repeat myself."

— Mark Twain
American Author
1835-1910

The Occupy Wall Street's complaint is economic inequality. The inequity manifests itself in many different locations, from Wall Street to Malibu. But there are two breeding grounds of inequity where the 99% still have clout: the U.S. House of Representatives and U.S. Senate.

The reality of being in the 99%. Our day-to-day financial obligations, the demands of our workplaces, the "rules" we are forced to work by — are viciously more unforgiving than the rules of conduct for our elected officials. There is no more blatant example of these inequities than in the U.S. Congress.

The U.S. Congress makes its own rules, thus they have cleverly crafted *very sketchy, wide-open* rules. As stated in Section 5 of the U.S. Constitution: *"Each House may determine the Rules of its Proceedings, punish its Members for disorderly Behaviour, and, with the Concurrence of two thirds, expel a Member."*

Section 5 of the U.S. Constitution was written in 1787. This document must be updated to protect the U.S. citizens of 2012. Why?
- The Senate and House are not capable of policing themselves.

- It's time to amend Section 5 for modern times.
- Section 5 has to be stricter, punishing absenteeism, revoking Congressional pay while campaigning, shortening campaign periods and terminating Congress's ability to get rich while in office.

Why do pols become so wealthy while they're in the Senate and House? Because they're privy to a virtual treasure trove of advance economic information. Fact is, they're *first* to learn about upcoming market shifts, failing industries and the awarding of government contracts. They get the news *first* and adjust their investments accordingly. Until recently, it's been perfectly legal for them to do so. Now it's not.

What if the Senate and House of Representatives had to show up for work? From 1789 to 1855, members of House of Representatives received a daily payment of $6.00 for showing up. Being paid for showing up was a smart system, because now, Senate and House members *don't show up!* If you watch CSPAN, notice the hollow chambers and sea of empty chairs.

The only member of Congress with a valid excuse for absenteeism is Gabrielle Giffords. As of this writing, Bobby L. Rush of Illinois has missed 10.7% of his voting responsibilities doing Constituent Work. Keith Ellison from Minnesota tore a knee tendon during a workout in the gym and missed over 10% of his votes. A bum knee is not an acceptable excuse in our world. In the private sector, where the 99% struggle under intractable rules, bosses will insist an employee return to work the day *after the birth of a child!*

Imagine, if you or I made a huge public announcement in our workplace – with balloons and a high school marching band - announcing our launch of a new job search, seeking more money and a promotion! What if we declared --- that during our job hunt --- we would not be showing up for work! Imagine making such an announcement, and still collecting our paychecks and benefits. Imagine! Our bosses would be throwing our belongings out the window and calling security. Yet U.S. elected officials get away with this year after year!

If you or I missed work because we were out looking for another job, we'd be fired immediately! But not in Washington. Michele Bachman, as of October 2011, missed 26% of House votes because she's been running for President. Same with Ron Paul, missing 69.7% of his voting responsibilities in the last quarter of 2011. Both savvy politicians are still picking up paychecks, even though they're not showing up for work and their focus is on their next job.

- **Any politician campaigning for their next job should not get paid for their current position**. All benefits should be curtailed while they're campaigning for their next political post. Better yet, they should be required to step down and forego their pay and benefits while campaigning *because campaigning while already in office is essentially job hunting.*

- **More rationally, political campaigns should be reduced to one month before an Election Day vote.** America's senselessly protracted, media-hyped campaigns do not produce the best candidates. Our current campaign system merely provides a platform for members of the 1% to argue with other members of the 1% over religion, female reproduction and boatloads of meaningless garbage that do not address the real problems of the 99%. These empty suits and their white-noise speeches, their baby-kissing and dog-petting and bible-thumping have nothing to do with crucial long-term changes necessary to bring America back.

- **Long, protracted political campaigning is only affordable for the 1%!** Long, expensive campaign marathons immediately eliminate members of the 99% from running for office. Because we can't afford years of campaigning! That's why we see all of those tired old "pol" faces again and again — *they have the bucks!* And now they have PACs. That's why the 99% are never accurately represented in Washington. The elected are 1%-ers, and they're protecting the interests of the 1%.

- Above all, these marathon campaigns prevent politicians from actually getting anything done on behalf of the 99%.

Nice salaries that only grow! Even though members of the House of Representatives and the Senate are not held to any standard test of accountability, they still make good money. They can stink at their jobs, and still, they're bringing home premium bacon. The current salary (2011) for rank-and-file members of the House and Senate is $174,000 per year. Their cost of living raise (COLA) automatically kicks-in, unless they vote to not accept their annual COLA. Miraculously, in 2011, they had the decency to turn down their COLA raise.

Leaders of the House and Senate are paid a higher salary! Senate Majority Party Leader - $193,400

Minority Party Leader - $193,400

House Leadership Speaker of the House - $223,500

Majority Leader - $193,400

Minority Leader - $193,400

Decent pay and wealth expansion while in office!
- The median personal wealth for members of House of Representatives grew to $911,510 in 2009, up from $785,515 in 2008, according to the Center for Responsive Politics.
- Nearly half of the members of House of Representatives are millionaires.
- The median wealth of a U.S. House member was $765,010 in 2009, up from $645,503 in 2008, according to the Center for Responsive Politics.

But let's get specific. Here are some of the politicians who've amassed the big bucks:

- U.S. Sen. Dianne Feinstein from California, reported a net worth of between $46 million and $108.1 million in 2010.
- U.S. Sen. Jay Rockefeller of West Virginia, reported a net worth of between $61.4 million and $136.2 million in 2010.
- U.S. Rep. Michael McCaul of Texas, reported a net worth of between $73.7 million and $201.5 million in 2010.
- U.S. Rep. Vern Buchanan of Florida, reported a net worth of as much as $366.2 million in 2010.

- U.S. Sen. Herb Kohl is one of 261 millionaire members of House of Representatives, according to an analysis of personal wealth conduct by the Center for Responsive Politics.
- U.S. Rep. Jared Polis of Colorado, reported a net worth of between $36.7 million and $285.1 million in 2010.

- U.S. Sen. Mark Warner of Virginia, reported a net worth of between $65.7 million and $283.1 million in 2010.

- U.S. Sen. John Kerry from Massachusetts, reported a net worth of between $182.8 million and $294.9 million in 2010.

- U.S. Rep. Jane Harman of California, reported a net worth of between $151.5 million and $435.4 million in 2010.

- U.S. Rep. Darrell Issa, of California, reported a net worth of between $156.1 million and $451.1 million in 2010.

Did any of these Congressional members turn down their paychecks due to their abundance of wealth?

Not that I can find! I've Googled it, I've even Alta-Vista-ed it, and I can't find one. I checked, and even rich boy John Kerry picked up his 2011 paychecks.

A prestigious job title, for life.

Even after a member of House of Representatives has been fired by the American voters, they get to keep their title. Former members of House of Representatives can ride on their former titles for years, doing speaking engagements and becoming lobbyists. They also get pensions based on the formula calculated for U.S. Government workers, *even if they only served 5 years.*

From Politician to Lobbyist *and back!*

One reason why our Senate and House of Representatives don't actually do anything to curb lobbying is because lobbying is their next job. Say a Senator doesn't get re-elected. No big deal, they become a consultant or lobbyist! They still get to stay in DC, they make at least $70,000 a year, go to the same parties, conferences, lunches and meetings while hanging out with their buddies and keeping their hand in the game.

What does this mean to the 99%?

It indicates we're naïve to think Congress will ever vote in our best interests! They're simply not going to vote to protect the 99% _because they belong to the 1%!_ So we have to fire many, many members of the current U.S. House of Representatives and Senate for not showing up for work, obstructing progress, job hunting, protecting the interests of the 1% and turning into millionaires while in office.

"I have been up to see the Congress and they do not seem to be able to do anything except to eat peanuts and chew tobacco, while my army is starving."

— Robert E. Lee
U.S. General
1807-1870

Chapter 3. The Myth of "Big Government."

Let's face it. The U.S. Government is already big. It's massive. The government is vast and full of unqualified people who got their posts via favors and paybacks among the 1%. So when politicians express their displeasure with "big government," they really don't mean *shrinking* the ranks of a system that helps them and their buddies. They just don't want anybody *curtailing their activities.* They don't want anybody *policing or imposing too many rules or regulations.*

"Big government" is actually Washington code for "regulative agencies."
That's why we don't see any huge victories from the EPA, the SEC, FDA, Homeland Security or the DEA. These are symbolic agencies that were created under public pressure, to create the illusion that the U.S. Government "regulates" the environmental offenders, Wall Street swindlers, immigration profiteers and drug peddlers--- but only *to a limited extent.*

Regulation is bad for the 1%.
For decades, politicians have tried to make 'regulation' a dirty word. When you listen to politicians warn voters about "big government" and regulation "taking away our freedom," it is rhetoric they deliberately use to scare us. What they're *really* saying is: "We don't want our big-time campaign contributors to get caught."

Regulation is good for the 99%. Most of the rich and powerful could care less about the environment, Wall Street heists, immigration and the war on drugs. That's why all of these regulatory agencies are under-funded and oftentimes thrown under the bus. They were never meant to succeed. So when you hear "reducing big government" it means reducing regulatory agencies. That's no good for you or I.

Regulation of American government, finance, food, energy, drugs and the environment are imperative. If you're still buying into the mantra of deregulation, you're being played. *Deregulation is what caused The Great Depression.* So haven't we learned that without regulation, lawlessness and looting will take place? Big business will steal the marrow from your bones if they're not regulated. Here are some examples of what's happened due to deregulation:

- Wall Street swindled the economy through the TARP "bail out." In the aftermath, the average Wall Street salary in 2010 was $361,330.
- We spend $300 billion a year on drugs. The drug companies are shilling 24-hours a day with moronic TV commercials, while offering physician kickbacks and being cited on countless criminal charges.
- The food companies and fast food restaurants are reluctantly adjusting their menus as our population swells like parade balloons. One third of our country's population is obese. And despite the astronomical leap in juvenile diabetes, the *Senate declared pizza a vegetable!*
- Coal companies continue to flatten the mountain ranges of West Virginia and Kentucky. Halliburton and/or BP was too cheap to spring for the proper gadget and ended up destroying the Louisiana coast's ecosystem.

Essentially, thanks to under funding and lack of manpower in most U.S. regulatory agencies, we, the 99% are becoming a bunch of poor, unemployed fat people on Lexapro, living in a poisoned environment that's making us sicker, but we can't be treated because we can't afford health insurance.

But I digress. For now, let's just focus on what needs to be done in Financial Regulation.

Set a fire under the U.S. Securities and Exchange Commission's Butt. If we had to pick one regulatory agency – just one – that must be completely re-engineered, it has to be the SEC. As they are now, they're letting Wall Street rob us blind. They didn't catch on to Bernie Madoff as he "made off" with stolen millions. They can't seem to derail Goldman Sachs, Bank of America or Capital One's various transgressions. The SEC just can't get the job done because *they have fewer than 4,000 employees.*

"What I found out from my dealings with the SEC over eight and a half years is that their people are totally untrained in finance; they're unschooled; they're un-credentialed. Most of them are just merely lawyers without any financial industry experience..."

—Harry Markopolos
Financial Analyst
(and the man who caught Bernie Madoff)

Last February, SEC chairwoman Mary Schapiro said that the agency doesn't have enough money to satisfactorily police Wall Street or draft new regulations required by the Dodd-Frank financial reform law." – The *Huffington Post* 12/23/11

The SEC needs a bigger budget and at least 10,000 employees, infiltrating every nook and cranny of the U.S. securities and exchange landscape. The SEC must be a snaggle-toothed Doberman. If the 99% insisted on empowering the SEC, fear would return to Wall Street.

Make High-Frequency Trading, Robo Trading and Algorithmic Trading Illegal. Also known as "black box" trading. Here, Wall Street and international securities exchanges have computers performing stock orders, automatically selecting the most advantageous aspect of a stock order, 24/7. This method of trading is responsible for the "flash crash" of May 6, 2010, when the Dow Jones had its 2nd largest point swing ever. And similar crashes keep happening. Black Box Trading is a force of volatility, so it's no good for the 99%.

Consumer Financial Protection Bureau. They are currently touting their initiative to make credit card solicitations easier for consumers to read. *That's not enough. We need this Bureau to monitor the crippling acts of Experian, TransUnion and Equifax.*

"[And] in fact, nearly one-quarter of credit reports were found to have serious errors, including false delinquencies," says Brian Emus, Illinois director of Public Interest Research Group. "Despite the fact that errors can harm your credit and lower your credit score, the bureaus have never once been held accountable for their mistakes."

Our credit rating is lowered by *whether we pay bills on time.* Shouldn't a credit rating be primarily based on whether you *ultimately paid things off?* For those who have paid off a mortgage or any big ticket item, our credit ratings should be primarily based on our responsible actions.

Want to lower unemployment? The 99% are penalized by sub par credit ratings. These unforgiving, unforgetting credit rating agencies have us by the you-know-whats. Saddled with lousy credit ratings, we can't qualify for jobs due to biased, inaccurate credit ratings by the big three credit bureaus. Hold them accountable!

Chapter 4. Education

"The mediocre teacher tells. The good teacher explains. The superior teacher demonstrates. The great teacher inspires."

— William Arthur Ward
American scholar, teacher, writer
1921-1994

"The three-yearly OECD Programme for International Student Assessment (PISA) report, which compares the knowledge and skills of 15-year-olds in 70 countries around the world, ranked the United States 14th out of 34 OECD countries for reading skills, 17th for science and a below-average 25th for mathematics." — AFP International News, 2010

U.S. Public education has stagnated. Our students are corralled around like cattle and tested repeatedly like lab rats. In Massachusetts, we have the MCAS, which tests the heck out of students. MCAS scores pinpoint the educators whose students are not progressing in Math and Reading. So to protect themselves, Massachusetts' teachers and schools are teaching students *how to succeed at taking the MCAS tests.* And at the end of the school year, once MCAS has pinpointed the weak educators, those mediocre teachers can't be fired, because they're protected by one of the most generous union contracts ever written. "No Child Left Behind" and various other lame initiatives with snappy tag lines have not effectively improved American students' math or reading skills. We've tried everything except putting the responsibility on the individual educators. It's time we did.

We pay more than any other country for public education. So why don't we have the smartest kids? Because most public school teachers are mediocre. They drone. They don't pay individual attention to each student. They're inconsistent. They're unimaginative. They don't excite kids about being in school, and they have an ironclad union protecting their mediocrity. Imagine getting a sweet deal like this:

- After a 2 or 3 year period, job security until retirement
- Free professional development courses
- Health and pension benefits for life
- The longer you teach, the more money you make
- Accountability isn't conclusively monitored

What job in the world offers a better deal than teaching in U.S. Public Schools? Not many. The U.S. Senate has a pretty good deal, but U.S. teachers have it even *better!* In the private sector, we can be fired in two seconds, for no real reason, without any recourse. *But not teachers!* Plus, members of American teachers unions only have to work eight hours a day, they get plenty of vacations and *summers off!*

Luckily, academics and the press are finally beginning to catch on to the fact that teachers are the pivotal key to improving education in America. And that mediocre teacher performance really needs to be rated so we can fire them. The article below appeared in *The New York Times* on January 6, 2012:

Big Study Links Good Teachers to Lasting Gains

WASHINGTON — Elementary- and middle-school teachers who help raise their students' standardized-test scores seem to have a wide-ranging, lasting positive effect on those students' lives beyond academics, including lower teenage-pregnancy rates and greater college matriculation and adult earnings, according to a new study that tracked 2.5 million students over 20 years.

The paper, by Raj Chetty and John N. Friedman of Harvard and Jonah E. Rockoff of Columbia, all economists, examines a larger number of students over a longer period of time with more in-depth data than many earlier studies, allowing for a deeper look at how much the quality of individual teachers matters over the long term.

"Everybody believes that teacher quality is very, very important," says Eric A. Hanushek, a senior fellow at the Hoover Institution at Stanford and longtime researcher of education policy. "What this paper and other work has shown is that it's probably more important than people think. That the variations or differences between really good and really bad teachers have lifelong impacts on children."

"If you leave a low value-added teacher in your school for 10 years, rather than replacing him with an average teacher, you are hypothetically talking about $2.5 million in lost income," said Professor Friedman, one of the coauthors. 1/6/2012 *The New York Times*

So let the teachers be rated on their performance! The standardized testing that reveals poorly performing teachers is helpful. But why not augment statistical findings with the critiques of people who know more about teacher abilities and performance than anyone else? Ask the people who can truly determine a good teacher from bad: *the students.*

Imagine, you and I, working for a service company, and we kept failing our clients. Our clients weren't meeting their targeted performance numbers. Truth be told, our clients found us to be lacking in imagination, energy and inspiration. Even more telling, our clients were significantly underperforming against rivals, despite our advice, coaching and constant lecturing.

Well, in the real world, you and I would be fired. There would be no "give them another year" or "they're doing the best they can." We'd be gone with no farewell party. That's how it works in the real world. But not in the American Public School system!

Mid-year, and at the end of the school year, students should be asked to fill out a questionnaire on each of their teachers. Coupled with student test scores and other measures, student evaluations would provide the extra dimension of clarity needed to sort the good teachers from bad. It would also make students feel more empowered. It's very depressing to be stuck with a bad teacher for a year, with no recourse. It's even more depressing to be stuck in a school full of mediocre teachers. A student evaluation would give students a voice, alleviate some of the hopelessness that comes with being locked in with a terrible teacher, and it would help keep kids in school.

For those who believe this would never work: students are the first ones to tell you who the good teachers are. Students *like* effective teachers. They unanimously *praise* teachers who give them the keys to understanding and accomplishment! And students are the first to recognize that a bad teacher means confusion, a lost year and falling behind. Students despise bad teachers and love good teachers. I'll bet you fondly remember your best teachers, and you probably still haven't forgiven the lousy ones. I haven't. *(Are you still out there, Mr. Maynard? Hope you're not teaching!)*

For those who are outraged by my educator rant: remember, the U.S. spends more per student than any other country. We're turning out teachers who don't know how to teach, yet teachers' union contracts prevent change. We pour money into sustaining an unmonitored group of employees who, paradoxically, are not as rigorously tested as their students.

"Public educators also receive generous benefits, including 'defined-benefit' pensions that do not require any contribution from the teacher. A career teacher, without ever having to contribute a nickel, can normally retire at age 55 and receive close to 70 percent of his or her salary for life. There are hundreds of thousands of retired teachers drawing annual pensions of $40,000 or more — many young enough to begin second careers."

—Frederick M. Hess, Hoover Institution [2004]

For those who think I'm anti-union, I'm not. The effectiveness of other American union-run professions is tops. But in the union-run *educational profession,* we have one of the world's most ineffectual educational systems. Throwing money at it isn't making it better. But evaluating and eliminating ineffective employees will improve quality. And because we're lagging in Math and Science, Math and Science teachers should be required to do an extra year of student teaching to ensure that they learn *how to teach.*

Why should we care? Because the General Electrics of the world will successfully lobby to procure Visas for foreigners who will in turn, fill American jobs. Our kids must be better educated in math and science in order to secure U.S. jobs. Otherwise, our kids will be saying "do you want that with fries?" for the rest of their lives.

The teaching profession must be held accountable. When you do a teacher's day, you realize teachers could never survive in the private sector – the private sector is far more difficult. For all the press and image rendering of the "self sacrificing public school teacher" – beneath that image is one very cushy profession that is failing its students, and ultimately failing our country. To learn more shocking facts, visit **www.teachersunionexposed.com** and write to the following groups:

The National Council of Teachers of Mathematics
1906 Association Drive
Reston, VA 20191-1502

National Science Teachers Association
1840 Wilson Boulevard
Arlington, VA 22201

The American Federation of Teachers AFL CIO
555 New Jersey Ave., NW
Washington, DC 20001

National Education Association
1201 16th Street, NW
Washington, DC 20036-3290

Chapter 5. Taxes

"It is well enough that people of the nation do not understand our banking and monetary system, for if they did, I believe there would be a revolution before tomorrow morning."

— Henry Ford
Founder, Ford Automobile Co.
Father of the Modern Assembly Line
1863-1947

Ever watch Sunday morning network television? General Electric fills our hi-def screens with stirring, expensively produced TV spots, declaring their deep abidance and commitment to people and all that is good in the world! And yet, General Electric doesn't pay U.S. taxes. Instead of paying taxes, they're marketing and lobbying.

If General Electric were an honorable American company, it would stop playing on public sentiments by airing emotional image TV spots. If GE were honorable, they would help the United States by paying taxes. And yet, through GE's high-powered legal/tax division, they tirelessly figure out ways for GE to avoid paying U.S. taxes via open loopholes in our tax code and offshore banking. Even so, GE brazenly uses our roads, relies on U.S. infrastructure and *exists* because of this fine country. So what should the 99% do to make GE start paying taxes again?

1. Boycott GE products
2. Ban GE from being awarded government contracts
3. Make offshore banking illegal for all U.S. companies and corporations

4.   Stop GE from sending jobs offshore and
        importing foreign employees on work visas

Write to Jeff Immelt, CEO of General Electric. He makes
over $15 million dollars a year, so he can figure out a way for
GE to do the honorable thing and pay taxes.

Jeff Immelt, CEO, General Electric Company
3135 Easton Turnpike
Fairfield CT 06828

The *New York Times* reports, "[since] 2002, the company
[General Electric] has eliminated a fifth of its work force in the
United States while increasing overseas employment."

Oh, just so you know, General Electric paid $235.2 million to
political groups (lobbyists and consultants) since 2000, and
has forked over zero federal income taxes in 2008, 2009, and
2010. But they paid $21,010,000.00 in lobbying fees in 2011.

"With the Obama administration drafting a corporate tax
reform plan, the report found General Electric, American
Electric Power Co. Inc., DuPont Co., and nine other companies
had a negative 1.5 percent tax rate on $171 billion in profits
over the three years studied."
                        -- Kevin Drawbaugh, *Huffington Post*, 6/2/11

80% of the largest U.S. corporations use offshore tax havens.
Here are others who've snaked their way out of paying taxes:

- Boeing (In Feb. 2011, was awarded a $35 BILLION
  dollar contract by the U.S. Air Force! They must have
  one heck of a lobby!)
- AIG (Received about $125 billion in TARP money and
  the Fed has about $39 billion invested in AIG)
- PG&E Corp (Made $1.1 billion in profits, 2010)

- Citicorp (received $20 billion in TARP bailout funds, October, 2011 reported profits of $3.8 billion)
- Carnival Corporation (September, 2011, reported $1.30 billion in net profits)
- Bank of America: With 115 offshore accounts, Bank of America paid no 2010 taxes, even though they had a $4.4 billion-dollar profit and took in $336 billion in TARP money in 2009.

"The *New York Times* captured the new corporate order succinctly in 1987, reporting that it 'eschews loyalty to workers, products, corporate structures, businesses, factories, communities, even the nation. All such allegiances are viewed as expendable under the new rules. With survival at stake, only market leadership, strong profits and a high stock price can be allowed to matter'."

— Barbara Ehrenreich, Author

What is the attraction of "offshore" bank accounts?
According to Jim Duggan, a partner at Chicago law firm Duggan Bertsch, "Diversification from our government, policies, and banking systems". The last few years have shaken faith in our system. Duggan says growing numbers of his clients are worried about the financial system, confiscation -- the whole shebang. "They're concerned about our government, and where our society is headed. There's a lot of socialistic tendencies, capital controls, the redistribution of wealth. -*The Wall Street Journal,* 2/13/12

Taxing Unemployment and Social Security Payments.

I always feel bad when witnessing the reaction of a 99%er when they first learn that their unemployment check and Social Security payments are going to be taxed. Most Americans are shocked by it. It's so contradictory to the very reason for furnishing relief funds. It's so dishonorable to the American worker. But Congress started taxing unemployment dollars during the 1980's under the Reagan administration. Today, it's time the 99% put an end to this theft.

Tax Church Property
Churches have gotten away with not paying taxes for a very long time under the guise of the separation between church and state. Yet today, religions are lobbying and actually meddling in legislation, including health care reform! They've stepped over the line, so it's time they paid taxes.

Write to: The National Taxpayers Union
108 Alfred St.
Alexandria, VA 22314

Just so you know what we're in for now:

Due to tax laws expiring this year and next, U.S. tax payers will owe $3,598 *more* in income tax in 2013 than in 2011 <u>with no increase in our incomes</u>. According to a piece by Bob Jennings, a CPA, EA and CFP and author of "*Understanding Social Security & Medicare,*" we're about to get hammered by taxes. Some of these items may have changed while this guide is being published, but here goes:

Major Individual Income Tax Benefits Expired 12/31/2011:

• Personal tax credits applied against income tax no longer apply

- Higher alternative minimum tax exemptions revert back to extraordinarily-low thresholds

- $250 school teacher expense deduction ends

- Mortgage insurance premium deduction expires

- State and local sales tax deductions expire

- Tuition and related fees deduction end

- IRA to charity tax-free transfers stop

- 2% Social Security tax reduction ends

Major Individual Income Tax Benefits Expired 12/31/2012:

- Marriage penalty equalization ends

- Dividends taxed at capital gains rates removed, taxed at regular rates now

- Capital gains low tax rates expires

- Removal of itemized deduction phase out for higher income Americans

- Removal of personal exemption phase out for higher income Americans

- Child care deduction limit of $3,000 reverts to $2,400

- Child credit reduces from $1,000 per child to $500 per child

- Low 10% tax bracket for low income Americans is eliminated

- Lower income tax rates and smaller brackets expires

- Refundable adoption credit and reduced deduction

- American Opportunity college education credit expires

• Major reduction in earned income credits and refunds

• Income tax exemption for debt forgiven on home foreclosures and repossessions

• Deduction for student loan interest ends

• Education IRA limit drops from $2,000 to $500

Other major changes for 2013, include a phase-out of itemized deductions and personal exemptions if income increases.

"For the 400 U.S. taxpayers with the highest adjusted gross income, the effective federal income tax rate-what they actually pay-fell from almost 30 percent in 1995 to just under 17 percent in 2007, according to the IRS. And for the approximately 1.4 million people who make up the top 1% of taxpayers, the effective federal income tax rate dropped from 29 percent to 23 percent in 2008. It may seem too fantastic to be true, but the top 400 end up paying a lower rate than the next 1,399,600 or so."

----How to Pay No Taxes
Jesse Drucker
Business Week, 4/15/11

Chapter 6. Immigration

"Any man who says he is an American, but something else also, isn't an American at all. We have room for but one flag, the American flag, and this excludes the red flag, which symbolizes all wars against liberty and civilization, just as much as it excludes any foreign flag of a nation to which we are hostile...We have room for but one language here, and that is the English language...and we have room for but one sole loyalty and that is a loyalty to the American people."

— Theodore Roosevelt
1858-1919
26th President of the United States

The Great Melting Pot has stopped melting. There's a lack of harmony within the U.S., because we are allowing so many different factions to proliferate and not assimilate.

We give immigrants no incentive to assimilate. The United States courts offer interpreters in the courtroom. We are required by law to print brochures in multiple foreign languages, despite the extra cost. Even the IRS offers a voice recording urging a caller to press "2" for Spanish. This is not what Teddy Roosevelt had in mind.

There are 11.2 million illegal immigrants in the U.S. today. How come? *We've made it easy for them to get in!*
- As of 2011, eight million members of the U.S. workforce are illegal immigrants
- U.S. Congress admits that immigration is a problem, yet our borders remain rife with gaping holes

What if we took a hiatus from immigration until we get the 99% back on track? It's a concept that bears discussion, because from 2000 to 2009, more than 10 million people were granted legal permanent resident (LPR) status in the United States. But now that our own established citizenry undergoes a horrific struggle to hang onto jobs, benefits and our homes, should we be taking in more citizens? The wise would say no.

The 99% come first. Politicians are callously watching the 99% struggle through catastrophic events in unemployment, foreclosure, loss of health insurance coverage, a hefty tax burden, spiraling national debt --- all of which are plunging the 99% into poverty. Meanwhile, legal and illegal immigrants enter our country, overwhelming our social support systems and derailing relief to the 99%. A hiatus from immigration until our citizens and economy are stabilized is a worthy idea.

We should be allowing immigration *only to the least populated states* which are Alaska, Wyoming, North and South Dakota. Scantily populated areas of states that could benefit from re-population would be improved by immigration. The states that are truly struggling to serve current populations, like California, Texas, Rhode Island and Nevada, should suspend all immigration. But listen to this --- In Rhode Island, *the Governor was actually considering granting drivers licenses to illegal immigrants!*

As for long-term illegal immigrants who have lived here in the United States for decades, we should grant them amnesty -- but send them to live in less populated states. Highly populated states and cities cannot afford to serve large illegal alien populations, particularly in metropolitan areas. There should be a price paid for illegal immigration, and living in a U.S. state that would benefit by population increase is a fair one.

We also must be more pragmatic about the skill levels of people we're immigrating. About each immigrant, we have to ask, will they be a burden to our already burdened population? Above all, we have to examine the real culprits of illegal immigration: *the countries that the illegal immigrants are leaving.*

Mexico and Central America:
62% of illegal aliens in the U.S. are from Mexico. While some immigrant populations actually contribute to U.S. productivity and economies, Mexican and Central American immigrants are far more likely to be low-skilled and less likely to speak English *or learn to speak English.*

As of [the effective date of this bill] July 20, 2011, only approximately 685 miles of the nearly 2,000 mile long border between the United States and Mexico is "fenced." The vast majority of this existing "fence" however, consists of barbed-wire, vehicle barriers, and inadequate materials that have minimal effectiveness in stopping illegal crossings. The approximately 1,315 remaining miles of the border currently have no fencing at all.

---www.Build the BorderFence.com

What can we do about it? We can build a frigging fence!
We can also repeal the North American Free Trade Agreement with Mexico. By reducing trade on the Texan-Mexican border, we'll also reduce the ability to cross our border. We must reinstate tariffs between Mexico and the U.S. Mexican farmers have only seen the price of their crops fall, making life even tougher for them, hence making them want to come here even more! Plus, you've got to admit, ever since NAFTA, we've seen U.S. manufacturing go right down the tubes.

"According to the Economic Policy Institute, rise in the trade deficit with Mexico alone since NAFTA was enacted led to the net displacement of 682,900 U.S. jobs by 2010."

Even better, we can stop giving Mexico money! We bailed Mexico out of a 1982 financial disaster. In 1995, we bailed Mexico out of an economic crisis with nearly $49 billion dollars. The Bush Administration gave Mexico 1.5 billion dollars in 2007 to fight drug trade and now, the drug wars have only intensified. This year, U.S. aid gave Mexico over $40 million dollars!

What does Mexico do with all the money we've given them? It's a good question, because Mexico still has a sketchy infrastructure and throat-choking pollution. It's still an undeveloped country with a staggeringly large impoverished, uneducated population and a fabulously wealthy upper 2%! Yet America continues to throw heaping sums of money at Mexico's perpetual indebtedness!

Brazil:
It's estimated that over 350,000 undocumented Brazilians are living in the U.S., primarily by overstaying lapsed Visas, then disappearing into large, metropolitan Brazilian neighborhoods and doing low wage work. It's estimated that over 70% of all Brazilians in the United States today are illegal immigrants.

So one would think, the U.S. would reduce the number of Visas granted to Brazilians, right? Not us! Instead, we're *including* Brazil in the U.S. Visa Waiver Program, permitting Brazilian travelers to come to the United States for 90 days without any Visa at all! Incidentally, the U.S. Visa Waiver Program has been amended with the support of Senator Barbara Mikulski of Maryland, but still. Who would okay something like this to begin with? A member of Congress succumbing to the American Hotel & Lodging Association Lobby, that's who. In 2011, they paid $1,235,576.00 in lobbying fees.

Asia and India: The fastest-growing population of illegal immigrants is Indian, and they're entering the United States while being smuggled through Guatemala and Mexico. Indians account for 2.3 percent of U.S. illegal immigrants. Guatemala has no specialized immigration laws, police, or court processes regarding immigrant trafficking, so Indians are easily transported through Central America into the U.S.! Doesn't sound like a big deal, but these are sophisticated, smart illegal aliens! In other words, they're gonna take our jobs.

Indian immigrants are educated. 39% of immigrant workers from Asia are in the professional or technical occupations. And while U.S. companies have job openings that *could be filled by unemployed U.S. citizens,* American companies are hiring immigrants instead of us! In 2006, 1.5 million Indian citizens came to the United States legally on employment-based visas, according to the U.S. Census. And yet, despite the fact that unemployment is one of this country's biggest problems, Representative Jason Chaffetz of Utah has introduced legislation to eliminate per country numerical limits for employment-based immigrants.

And while I've been writing this manifesto, Washington has been approving more trade agreements (South Korea and Columbia) to steal jobs from the U.S. and create even tighter offshore tax havens in Panama. Those in the know are calling the South Korean and Columbian deals "NAFTA on steroids."

Clearly, Washington's allegiances are not with you and I.

Visit **www.carryingcapacity.org** and write to:

U.S. Citizenship and Immigration Services, 500 12th Street SW, Washington, D.C. 20521-6050

NOMINATED THE BEST JOKE OF THE YEAR, 2011
A Russian arrives in New York City as a new immigrant to the United States. He stops the first person he sees walking down the street and says," Thank you Mr. American for letting me come into this country, giving me housing, food stamps, free medical care, and a free education!" The passerby says, "You are mistaken, I am a Mexican." The man goes on and encounters another passerby. "Thank you for having such a beautiful country here in America ." The person says, "I not American, I Vietnamese." The new arrival walks farther, and the next person he sees he stops, shakes his hand, and says, "Thank you for wonderful America !" That person puts up his hand and says, "I am from Middle East . I am not American." He finally sees a nice lady and asks, "Are you an American?" She says, "No, I am from Africa ." Puzzled, he asks her, "Where are all the Americans?" The African lady checks her watch and says, "Probably at work."

Chapter 7. Health Care

"We can always count on the Americans to do the right thing, after they have exhausted all the other possibilities."
—Sir Winston S. Churchill
1874-1965
Former Prime Minister of Great Britain

First, the United States is the *only* major country on the planet that attaches health care to employment. No other big time country does this. Just us.

"A [second] major shortcoming of employment-based health insurance is that it is only temporary. It is tied to a particular job in a particular company, and it is lost with that job. Nowhere else in the industrialized world does a family, already down on its luck over a job loss, also suffer the loss of its health insurance. It happens only in America, under employment-based insurance." — *Uwe E. Reinhardt is an economics professor at Princeton. From The New York Times, 5/22/2009*

The 99% know that health care can no longer be attached to employment. That's because we've been unemployed, under employed or self employed. As a result, we understand that if you're unemployed, it's likely you don't have health care. We understand the implications of that tenuous connection. But the 1% --- for whom the employment/health insurance connection is working just fine – they're obstructing health care reform.

— About 45,000 Americans die each year because they don't have health care insurance coverage

— Around 700,000 Americans go bankrupt each year because of medical bills

Doing something about health care shows progress. Politicians can bark and whine about "Obamacare" but at least Obama is attempting to improve health care for the 99%. Nonetheless, Obama's people came up with an incredibly complex, two thousand page document weighed down with a mandate legally requiring Americans to buy health insurance. Over time, the size of the document has been reduced to under 900 pages. But still. Why is this taking so long?

Health care reform is now in the hands of the U.S. Supreme Court, further delaying health care coverage for me and 50.7 million other uninsured Americans. Now we have to wait until June, 2012 to learn the Supreme Court's ruling.

Let me tell you how the health care "mandate" has worked out in Massachusetts. I can't afford health insurance, *but now I have to pay a fine for not having health insurance.* That's how helpful the mandate is for the 99%. The fee can be as high as $1,212.00 a year for those over 27 making $32, 676.00 a year.

Fact is, if the authors of public policy would just create a simple, inexpensive, high-quality health care alternative, no mandate would be necessary.

Offer decent health care coverage for the 99% and you won't need a mandate.
- Our health care should be simple, high-quality and about $100 a month per person, $200 for a family of 4.

- It should include dental, since health researchers are linking multiple health conditions, like heart disease, to dental deterioration.
- The American health care act should be 100 pages in length, easy to understand, and without a mandate.
- Health care reform should be achieved by the end of 2012, it should be in effect immediately — not in 2014. The 99% can't wait that long.

We. Still. Don't. Have. Health Care Reform. *Still!*
It's inexcusable. The Senate, the House of Representatives, the politicians, office holders ---- they can't seem to find a solution despite decades of panels, task forces, debates, discussions, feasibility studies, summits, czars and surveys. They can't seem to come up with a plan, even though they have a virtual treasure trove of working examples from other countries' approaches to health care!

France: This older, wiser country offers government-financed, universal health care and is ranked as one of the world's best health care systems.

Norway & Sweden: At the top of worldwide health care ratings, Norway offers a universal public health system to its entire population, paid largely from taxation.

United Kingdom: Offers a National Health Service to all UK permanent residents, free at the point of need and paid for via general taxation. Citizens can also buy private health care insurance.

Hong Kong: Offers a combination of public and private hospitals. Includes dental care as part of overall health care coverage in their national Department of Health. The national Hospital Authority monitors hospital compliance.

<u>Switzerland</u>: Switzerland's government spending on health care is the lowest in the developed world while they offer the highest quality health coverage in the world. Their Universal Coverage for all citizens is provided by regulated private insurers and includes dental care.

Swiss health care coverage has an individual mandate. It's a highly regulated system, not attached to employment, and 99.5% of all Swiss citizens are covered by health insurance. And they're able to accomplish all this while co-existing with a Swiss national health care lobby. 'Nuff said.

Who else is standing in the way of Health Care Reform? Paid corporate lobbyists.

Blue Cross/Blue Shield paid $15,855,834 in lobbying fees in 2011. And Blue Cross/Blue Shield isn't the only U.S. health player paying big time lobby bucks to stand in the way of health care reform. The American Medical Association forked over $16,190,000 in lobbying expenses in 2011, joined by The American Hospital Association chiming in with $14,060,000.00 (2011). No wonder health care is so expensive! Imagine if that money was re-routed to actually lower the cost of health care?

Congressional stalling tactics and unwillingness to embrace even the tiniest measures to reform health care have completely mired progress. Plus, the Catholic lobby has gotten involved (despite the so-called separation of church and state) just to bring progress to a total standstill. For those of us who desperately need affordable health care, these delays are unacceptable.

"Catholic bishops said Friday night that they would not support the Obama administration's proposed compromise on a controversial rule that requires most employers to fully cover contraception in their workers' health plans."

-The Wall Street Journal, 2/12/12

The Health Care Lobby must be eliminated. Republican, Democrat, Libertarian, Tea Party, Justice Party – whoever you are, lobbyists need to be blocked from messing with our health care system. It interferes with the provision of adequate health care coverage to the American people. The lack of affordable health care isn't just holding back individuals, it's pulled a straightjacket over American small businesses. It prevents small business from hiring older, unemployed Americans.

"...the group health-insurance premiums employers pay to private insurers are "experience rated" over that employer's group of employees. This means that the group premium is based on the claims experience – that is, the health history — of just that small group of employees. For small employers, it can mean that if serious illness befalls one or several employees in the group, it can drastically and unpredictably drive up the premium for every employee in the group."

— *Uwe E. Reinhardt, The New York Times, 5/22/2009*

Health care access and affordability has been an issue in this country for more than 67 years. It's so clear what the 99% need – simple, affordable health insurance that is not attached to employment, that doesn't penalize small business and supports the overall health of the nation. I can't afford health care and I can't wait for provisions to finally take place in 2014. Americans need affordable, flexible health care NOW. *Why is this so impossible to achieve?*

Imagine, you and I in a workplace where we've been told what to do yet we just don't do it. How long would we last? We'd be fired in 2 weeks. And yet, in the cushy workplace of Congress, politicians continue to stammer out excuses. So please don't re-elect them!

Ever watch old movies? I love watching "American Graffiti," "Beach Blanket Bingo," "Bye Bye Birdie," "Jaws"... Sure, the stories are classic and they depict a teenage America of yesteryear, but when you look at old films, you realize how thin and healthy American teenagers used to be! Obesity was a rarity. Now when I drop off my kid at the high school, I see 300-pound teenagers struggling to walk, 15-year-old girls weighing in at 185 and kids with absolutely no muscle tone. And when I go to the Parent/Teacher conferences, the parents are even fatter. But nothing tops the tragedy of subbing in classrooms where little kids are so over weight, they can't fit in the elementary school-sized chairs.

Obesity is a real crisis. Today, roughly one third of America is obese. 190 million fat people. In 2008, $147 billion dollars was spent on treating obesity-related ailments, according to The U.S. Centers for Disease Control and Prevention. And that's an old number. Can you imagine how much it's going to cost next year?

Weigh-in on this. American obesity is raising the cost of health care. If you think I'm being callous, I counter with the fact that we, as a people, have been far too lenient about weight and obesity.

"An obese person will have an average of $8,315 in medical bills a year in 2018 compared with $5,855 for an adult at a healthy weight. That's a difference of $2,460."
  — Kenneth Thorpe, chairman of the Department of Health Policy and Management at Emory University in Atlanta

Fat food. And what's the story with American restaurant chains? How honorable is it for them to continually serve unbelievably fatty, sugary and salt drenched food?

The Denny's Midwestern Meat and Potatoes Sandwich:
Grilled prime rib and French fries smothered in brown gravy and topped with melted Swiss and American cheeses and mayo. Served on a Cheddar bun with a side of mashed potatoes and gravy.
2,050 Mgs of salt! 118 carbohydrates! 18 grams of saturated fat!

Fat food restaurants and companies should be fined. But last year, McDonald's paid $988,160 in lobbying fees, so fat chance any member of Congress will stand up to them. No honor among thieves — ain't it the truth! But luckily, Darden Restaurants is an honorable company:

September 15, 2011
Darden Restaurants' Plans to Reduce Calorie, Sodium Footprint
The Nation's Leading Restaurant Brands Debut Plans to Offer Greater Choice and Variety

WASHINGTON, Sept. 15, 2011 /PRNewswire-USNewswire/ -- Darden Restaurants, the world's largest full-service restaurant company, whose brands include Red Lobster, Olive Garden, LongHorn Steakhouse and Bahama Breeze, today announced the most comprehensive health and wellness commitment in the restaurant industry to date. Darden has committed to reduce its calorie and sodium footprints and to provide greater choice and variety on its children's menus.

For the health of the 99%, please send your letters to:

The U.S. Senate Committee on Health Education Labor and Pensions, 428 Senate Dirksen Office Building, Washington DC 20510

Tom Harkin (IA), Barbara A. Mikulski (MD),Jeff Bingaman (NM),Patty Murray (WA),Bernard Sanders (I) (VT),Robert P. Casey, Jr. (PA),Kay R. Hagan (NC),Jeff Merkley (OR),Al Franken (MN),Michael F. Bennet (CO),Sheldon Whitehouse (RI),Richard Blumenthal (CT), Michael B. Enzi (WY),Lamar Alexander (TN),Richard Burr (NC),Johnny Isakson (GA),Rand Paul (KY),Orrin G. Hatch (UT), John McCain (AZ),Pat Roberts (KS),Lisa Murkowski (AK),Mark Kirk (IL)

House Ways and Means Committee Office
1102 Longworth House Office Building
Washington D.C. 20515
Wally Herger, CA, Chairman

Sam Johnson, TX

Paul Ryan, WI

Devin Nunes, CA

Dave Reichert, WA

Peter Roskam, IL

Jim Gerlach, PA

Tom Price, GA

Vern Buchanan, FL

Fortney Pete Stark, CA
Mike Thompson, CA
Ron Kind, WI
Earl Blumenauer, OR
Bill Pascrell, Jr., NJ

Council for Affordable Health Insurance
127 S. Peyton Street, Suite 210
Alexandria, VA 22314

The U.S. Dept. of Health & Human Services
200 Independence Ave., SW
Washington, D.C. 20201

"We should resolve now that the health of this nation is a national concern; that financial barriers in the way of attaining health shall be removed; that the health of all it's citizens deserves the help of all the nation."

—Harry S. Truman
1884-1953
33rd President of the United States

Chapter 8. Alternative Energy

The 99% is well aware that the U.S. must switch over to solar, wind and alternative energy sources. But the 1% tells us – the 99% -- that we must cut back our oil consumption. The 1% doesn't understand that the American economy, environment and standard of living would vastly improve if we left fossil fuels behind.

Fossil fuels are finite. We've based the primary fuel of our nation for heat, travel and industry on an energy source that *is going to run out*. Not our fault. There was a time when we thought fossil fuels were abundant and cheap. That's no longer true. So what are we doing here, cowtowing to Big Oil?

Our political decision makers still turn a blind eye to alternative renewable energy development because of the powerful Big Oil, Coal and Natural Gas lobbies' influence. They're so blind to alternative energy that China is now the leader in the solar and wind power industries. Our lawmakers are under the spell of the oil and gas lobbies. So much so, they're sticking to tax breaks for Big Oil and they're still pushing for the XL Keystone pipeline running from Canada to the Texas.

"This U.S. Senate has to stop looking towards the past and move into the new century. If only some of these politicians showed the same level of passion for creating new markets around cleaner forms of energy, as they're showing for crippling a sitting president with a dirty, potentially highly dangerous, old-school Canadian tar sands pipeline."

– Robert Redford,
American Actor
Environmental Activist
[2/13/12]

We can't afford fossil fuels. It is perhaps one of the biggest shams of all time that we are not using free sources of renewable energy --- the sun, the wind --- to run our cars, heat our homes and power our machines. Energy costs drive up the cost of EVERYTHING, from college tuitions to American manufacturing. Energy costs from fossil fuels have our nation in a stranglehold. And yet, our Congress keeps behaving as though renewable energy is something destined for a faraway century – when we'll be living in space ships and vacationing on the moon.

Environmental damage. From the Exxon Valdez to BP's Louisiana off shore drilling disaster, oil is messy stuff. There is no such thing as clean coal – coal is a dirty business. The coal people are so ruthless, they cut off the tops of mountains to extract coal. Gas lines explode. We don't know where to put nuclear waste. *So why are we still messing with this stuff?*

The myth of fracking. And while natural gas is enjoying lower prices and a new abundance, it's still a short-term solution. Same with fracking [trying to extract oil from shale in Colorado, Utah and Wyoming].

Here's one account of "fracking" technology:
"Getting petroleum-like substances out of oil shale, which is first mined, is tougher than pumping oil out of traditional wells, and companies haven't found an economic way to do it. In the U.S. Oil shale contains kerogen, which must be subjected to temperatures of more than 750 degrees before it can produce oil. Studies have indicated up to about 500 gallons of water may be needed to produce one barrel of oil from it, which could be an issue in the dry West, the Government Accountability Office has said."

-The Huffington Post, 2/4/12

Here's another description of "fracking":

"...the reserves are usually about five kilometres below the surface (much deeper than coal seam gas); wells are drilled down to them and then horizontally through them for another 5 or 6 kilometres; the horizontal part of the well is perforated by explosives and then fluid and sand are pumped down at high pressure to fracture the shale. The hydrocarbons then flow to the surface."

—Alan Kohler
Australian Broadcasting Company

Solar and Wind are ready to go, and they're a heck of a lot simpler than fracking! They don't waste water. They don't require explosives. They don't damage the environment. Solar and wind power are no longer fictional projections from a Jetsons cartoon. They're ready to be deployed now. We have the scientific know-how and engineering capabilities to replace oil, coal and gas with wind and solar. So why isn't Congress moving on a complete shift from oil, coal and gas to solar, wind and electric? Wager a guess that the delay has to do with the lobbying force field of Big Oil, foreign policy and pure profiteering.

Alternative energy now. The next set of elected officials must be convinced to make alternative, renewable energy sources priority #1. Relying on wind and solar will lower the operating costs of everything for everybody.

Write and give your support to:
The Union of Concerned Scientists National Headquarters
2 Brattle Square, Cambridge MA 02138-3780

Share your displeasure with:
Rex W. Tillerson, Chairman and CEO
Exxon Mobil Corp. (World's most profitable company, 2011)
5959 Las Colinas Boulevard
Irving, TX 75039

"The use of solar energy has not been opened up because the oil industry does not own the sun."

Ralph Nadar
American Political Activist
1934 —

Chapter 9. Paid Corporate Lobbying

"Ten people who speak make more noise than ten thousand who are silent."

— Napoleon Bonaparte
Emperor of France
1769-1821

It's not "big government" bringing Beltway progress to a standstill – it's lobbying. Lobbying is like Tolkien's character "Gollum" in *Lord of the Rings*. Feed it, and it gets bigger and more powerful and more insidiously manipulative. Paid corporate lobbying screws with the minds and sensibilities of Congress, 'til everyone is drooling over their bank statements, chanting, *"precious, precious!"* Lobbying casts a pall over Washington D.C. and whispers tempting propositions that prevent crucial reforms.

Widen the definition of Lobbying. Right now, lobbying is defined by a lobbyist physically walking up to a member of Congress and asking them to vote on behalf of their lobby's concerns. That definition isn't casting a wide enough net. Because right now, we have powerful Washington consultants who are doing everything *except* physically talking to a member of Congress on behalf of their lobby, but they're not paying lobbying registration fees. For example, a current candidate for U.S. President made $55 million dollars in *consulting* on behalf of health care --- but he's not *technically* lobbying because he didn't actually *physically* take a request to a member of Congress. So technically, he's not a lobbyist. Yeah, right. This fact was revealed this morning in an NPR news report.

It is travesties like this one (above) that reveal the destructive power of lobbying:

"The United States House of Representatives voted to rebuke new U.S.D.A. guidelines for school lunches that would have increased the amount of fresh fruit and vegetables in school cafeterias, and instead, declared that the tomato paste on frozen pizza qualified it as a vegetable. For this we can thank large food companies -- in this case ConAgra and Schwan -- which pressured House of Representatives to comply with their financial interests." -*The Huffington Post*, 11/19/11

Voting pizza as a vegetable demonstrates how Lobbying defies the interests of the 99%. Because of paid corporate lobbying and hefty campaign donations, our Senators and House of Representatives keep corporate tax loopholes wide open for big U.S. corporations to squirrel their way out of paying taxes. Federal contract awards are firmly influenced by lobbyists. That's why Boeing still scores lucrative Government contracts although they don't pay U.S. taxes.

Instead of standing up to lobbyists and saying "Pizza is not a vegetable!" our elected officials typically will do the following: form a task force. They'll send out a press release and the politicians will be photographed with an ethnically diverse bunch of children holding pizza slices. They'll hire an ad agency to write a clever tag line and produce some television public service announcements that will air at 2:00 a.m., *but they'll still vote that pizza is a vegetable.*

Elected officials can't protect the 99%'s best interests while under the influence of lobbyists. And while initiatives have been passed to monitor lobbying, lobbying expands. Lobbyists fight regulation. They represent the major U.S. companies who don't pay taxes. They twist inconceivable laws into place and keep the 1% employed.

The Lobby is where out-of-work politicians, educators, political staffers and former advisors go. Of course the Beltway is going to support lobbying – *it's their back-up job plan.* Where do you think the former Chief of Staffs of the world fester when they're not on a presidential staff? They're lobbying! Here's an example of how the dust settles after each administration changes:

> "Nicholas Calio, Citigroup's top lobbyist, handled congressional relations for both the first and second President George Bush. Its [Citigroup's] team of outside lobbyists has also included a former congressional liaison for President Clinton, a former chairman of the Federal Deposit Insurance Corporation, a former deputy assistant Treasury secretary and the veteran Democratic strategist Steve Elmendorf." - *The New York Times*, 1/23/09

You and I wonder why Congress doesn't accomplish more. Well, they're spending time being lobbied, at the most amazing restaurants, fabulous parties and vacation destinations in the world! They're playing golf. They're being wined and dined. All the while, they're still picking up their paychecks! And if they're not at the party, they're *throwing* the party in order to fundraise for their next campaign! To learn about your representatives' party plans, visit:http://politicalpartytime.org

Instead of paying tax dollars, U.S. companies are paying lobbyists.
Today, there are 11,140 registered lobbyists in Washington, D.C., making between $79,374 and $136,240 a year. That's good money. This information comes from: http://www1.salary.com/Lobbyist-...

<u>From the Lobbying Requirements Website:</u>

*A lobbying firm is exempt from registration for a particular client if its total income from that client for **lobbying activities** does not exceed and is not expected to exceed $3,000 during a quarterly period. An organization employing in-house lobbyists is exempt from registration if its total expenses for **lobbying activities** do not exceed and are not expected to exceed $11,500 during a quarterly period.*

Want to lower the U.S. deficit? Limit paid corporate lobbyists to 500 players a year and charge top dollar [in the multi-million to billion-dollar range] to be at the table. Our national debt could melt away if we'd increase paid corporate lobbying registration fees. Just to strengthen the point, how much did GE lobbyists pay the U.S. Government to register to lobby our House of Representatives? Good question. Can't find an answer. But boy, it would be interesting to find out.

Even during the 2008 banking crisis, the banks did not cease their lobbying.
"During the last three months of 2008, at least seven [other] firms receiving bailout funds — American Express, Capital One, Goldman Sachs, KeyCorp, Morgan Stanley, PNC and Bank of New York Mellon — all lobbied the government about the bailout, according to a review of their most recent disclosure reports." *The New York Times* 1/23/09

<u>Support anti-lobbying groups like:</u>
Common Cause, 1133 19th St. NW, Washington DC 20036
www.commoncause.org

<u>These are addresses where lobbying filing documents are sent:</u>

Office of the Clerk
The U.S. House of Representatives
The Capitol, Room H-154

Washington DC 20515-6601

Senate Office of Public Records
232 Hart Senate Office Building
Washington, DC 20510

Legislative Resource Center
B-106 Cannon House Office Building
Washington, DC 20515

Senate Office of Public Records
232 Hart Senate Office Building
Washington, DC 20510

"It cannot be seen, cannot be felt,
Cannot be heard, cannot be smelt,
It lies behind stars and under hills,
And empty holes it fills,
It comes first and follows after,
Ends life, kills laughter."

—J.R.R. Tolkien, Author
1892-1973
Author of The Hobbit & Lord of the Rings

Chapter 10. Political Parties

"Somewhere along the way, someone is going to tell you, 'There is no "I" in team.' What you should tell them is, 'Maybe not. But there is an "I" in independence, individuality and integrity.'" And if they tell you you're not a team player, congratulate them on being observant."

— George Carlin
American Comedian
1937-2008

Partisan politics and party arm wrestling has brought this country to its knees.

- Regardless of your political preferences, none of us can afford to blindly vote straight down party lines anymore. We can only vote for the most *effective* person for the job – people with proven track records of getting things done on behalf of the best interests of the 99%.

"Ours is a system focused not on collective problem-solving but on a struggle for power between 2 private organizations."
— Mickey Edwards, The Atlantic, August 2011

- Face the facts. Republicans are so busy trying to prove how conservative they are, while Democrats are trying to prove how liberal they are – both persuasions can't work together. A politician's staunch allegiance to a single political party virtually guarantees nothing but future stalemate, so don't vote for them. They won't get anything done.

- Accountability and progress – *that is relevant*. That's worth a vote. Think of yourself as a hiring manager. Would you hire a slick charmer with a Marie Antoinette hairstyle, porcelain fingernails and gleaming shoes who insists he's right for the job because he's big into religion, he's concerned about women's reproduction, and he's great guy to have a beer with? As a hiring manager, I'd be showing that guy to the door. He hadn't proven himself at all! And yet, we put people in office based on that thin scenario.

The "myth" of Unenrolled voting status. In an effort to prevent voters from registering as Independents, they've changed the name of Independent voting status to "Unenrolled." This is deliberately designed to scare people from registering as Independent voters! Don't be fooled. Registering as "Unenrolled" means you're an Independent and you can vote however you want in the next election. And that's perfectly okay. It's your right as a U.S. voter.

Imagine, if you and I were so doggedly entrenched in a philosophical difference with a fellow employee, that all we did was fight? What if we fought so frequently and were so embroiled in argument that we never got anything done? Well, in any company --- from the local grocery store to the upper echelons of the highest skyscrapers – we'd be fired. Apply that thinking to anyone who is running for office. If your candidate is completely immersed in party politics, they're not going to get anything done.

We shop online, we communicate online, we go to college online. Why can't we vote online? We don't have to make people go out in the rain and punch a ballot. We don't have to make voters show a special I.D. card. That's backwards thinking. The fact is, our dated voting system actually *discourages* people from voting! And if some naysayer worries about voter fraud online, remember, our existing voting system is full of opportunities for fraud! Remember the "hanging chads" of Florida? Our technology has undergone a quantum shift to the internet, and yet we're still using an antiquated method of voting. It doesn't make sense.

Think how easy it would be to vote online. More people would vote if we eliminated our prehistoric system of voting. We could dump electoral voting --- because electoral voting was a solution for 1787 – not 2012. Caucuses and electoral votes deserve some new thinking. It's high time to amend electoral voting in article II, section 1 of the Constitution.

Declare yourself an Independent.
If the 99% re-registered their party affiliations as Independents (unenrolled), *it would scare the heck out of both political parties. And both parties have become so arrogant and uncaring about the fate of the 99%, they deserve a bit of a scare.*

A dramatic shift to Independent voter affiliation would be the most powerful statement we could possibly make as voters. And it would actually be a much-needed slap on the side of Washington's collective, well-coiffed heads. Plus you can still vote for whomever you want.

Visit www.independentvoting.org!

"It's not whether you got knocked down; it's whether you get back up."

— Vince Lombardi
American Football Coach
1913-1970

11. **Layoff the U.S. Congress**

"It is the first responsibility of every citizen to question authority."

— Benjamin Franklin
Founding Father of the United States
1706-1790

It's so tiresome, the way all political parties keep dragging out the same craggy old faces, year after year. *Their hair and their dental work look great.* Their suits are flawless. They speak in commanding voices and can even work-up a tear while saying the Pledge of Allegiance. But they're running for the 1%, not you and I.

So let's fire them. After all, you and I hired them. In the following pages, I've included names and addresses of some committees, but not all. You can get more information at **www.house.gov** or **www.senate.gov** to zero- in on the committees that have let you down.

Let's hold Congress to the same workplace standards that you and I are subject to. If you or I were head of the Senate Banking and Finance Committee, we would have been fired by now. Let's demand their resignations by mailing each of these employees at:

The U.S. Senate Committee on Banking, Housing and Urban Affairs, Room SD G06, Dirksen Senate Office Building, Washington DC 20510-6075

Tim Johnson of South Dakota, Chairperson

Jack Reed of Rhode Island
Charles E. Schumer of New York
Robert Menendez of New Jersey
Daniel K. Akaka of Hawaii [up for re-election in 2012!]
Sherrod Brown of Ohio [up for re-election in 2012!]
Jon Tester of Montana
Herb Kohl of Wisconsin
Mark R. Warner of Virginia
Jeff Merkley of Oregon
Michael F. Bennet of Colorado
Kay R. Hagan of North Carolina

Budget Committee
This is a useless committee because Congress appears to be
unable to keep to a budget. Above all, they keep giving money
to the wrong people. A lot of this committee is up for re-
election, so let's ask them why they can't seem to stick to a
budget or accomplish anything?

The U.S. Senate Budget Committee
Main Office, 624 Dirksen Senate Office Building
Washington DC 20510

Kent Conrad of North Dakota, Chairman [and up for re-
election in 2012!]
Patty Murray of Washington
Ron Wyden of Oregon
Bill Nelson of Florida [up for re-election in 2012!]
Debbie Stabenow of Michigan [up for re-election in 2012!]
Benjamin L. Cardin of Maryland [up for re-election in 2012!]
Bernard Sanders of Vermont [up for re-election in 2012!]
Sheldon Whitehouse of Rhode Island [up for re-election in
2012!]
Mark R Warner of Virginia
Jeff Merkley of Oregon
Mark Begich of Alaska

Christopher Coons of Delaware

The Select Committee on Ethics. Here's what this committee needs to learn.

- Protracted political campaigns are unethical because the cost of these campaigns bar average-earning Americans from running for office.

- It's unethical for members of Congress to not show up or campaign for their next job while still in office.

- Congress members should be limited to being lobbied 3 hours a week and they should keep time logs.

- It's unethical for members of Congress worth more than $1 million dollars to collect a paycheck.

- It is unethical for politicians to become lobbyists and lobbyists to become politicians.

So let's tell these folks we need stricter Congressional ethics: Mail to: Senate Select Committee on Ethics, United States Senate, Room SH-220 Hart Building, Washington DC 20510

- Barbara Boxer of California
- Mark L. Pryor of Arkansas
- Sherrod Brown of Ohio (up for re-election in 2012)
- Johnny Isakson of Georgia
- Pat Roberts of Kansas
- James E. Risch of Idaho

The Special Committee on Aging

Let's tell this committee to protect the elderly from the hardscrabble poverty they are now experiencing due to the economic downturn.

- Medicare and Social Security are off the table. Do not touch them. Again: DO. NOT. TOUCH. SOCIAL. SECURITY. Or you'll never see in the inside of the Capitol Building again (unless you're on a tour).

- Fuel and heating assistance to the elderly must be increased, not reduced.

- The elderly should receive a 50% discount on utilities such as water, electricity, cable and telephone service.

- Big Pharma is gouging the elderly with the cost of prescription drugs.

Guess what? *All* of the following Congress members are up for re-election! Their address is: The U.S. Senate Special Committee on Aging, G31, Dirksen Senate Office Building, Washington DC 20510

- Herb Kohl of Wisconsin is the Committee Chairman
- Bill Nelson of Florida
- Robert P. Casey, Jr. of Pennsylvania
- Claire McCaskill of Missouri
- Sheldon Whitehouse of Rhode Island
- Kirsten E Gillibrand of NY
- Joe Manchin III of West Virginia
- Bob Corker of Tennessee
- Orrin Hatch of Utah
- Dean Heller of Nevada

Not up for re-election, but worthy of your criticism:
- Ron Wyden of Oregon
- Michael Bennet of Colorado
- Mark Udall of Colorado
- Richard Blumenthal of Connecticut
- Susan Collins of Maine
- Mark Kirk of Illinois
  Jerry Moran of Kansas
- Ron Johnson of Wisconsin
- Richard Shelby of Alabama
- Lindsey Graham of South Carolina
- Saxby Chambliss of Georgia

Joint Economic Committee

Whatever the Joint Economic Committee has been doing, they sure haven't improved the economy! Good news is, they're all up for re-election. Their address is: The U.S. Senate Joint Economic Committee, Room G-01, Dirksen Senate Office Building, Washington DC 20510

- Robert P. Casey, Jr. of Pennsylvania, Chairman is up for re-election in 2012
- Jeff Bingaman of New Mexico is up for re-election in 2012.
- Amy Klobuchar of Minnesota, up for re-election in 2012.
- Jim Webb of Virginia, up for re-election in 2012.
- Bernard Sanders of Vermont is up for re-election in 2012.

Not up for re-election, but worthy of your comments
Mark R. Warner, Virginia

Jim DeMint of South Carolina
Daniel Coats of Indiana
Mike Lee of Utah
Patrick Toomey of Pennsylvania

Joint Committee on Taxation

These guys treat you and I like doormats, so let's give them some marching orders! Send your mail (and lots of it!) ordering them to:

- Raise taxes on the 1%
- Increase taxes on U.S. Corporations who manufacture outside the U.S., import foreign workers via U.S. Work Visas, and practice foreign outsourcing
- Make the taxation of Social Security illegal
- Make the taxation of Unemployment benefits illegal
- All U.S. Corporations must be legally required to pay U.S. Taxes
- All members of Congress must be legally required to pay U.S. Taxes
- Tax churches

The Joint Committee on Taxation,1625 Longworth House Office Building, Washington, DC 20515

- Max Baucus of Montana
- John D. Rockefeller IV of West Virginia
- Kent Conrad of North Dakota [Up for re-election in 2012!!!!]
- Chuck Grassley of Iowa
- Orrin G. Hatch of Utah [Up for re-election in 2012!]
- Dave Camp, *Chairman*, Michigan
- Wally Herger, California
- Sam Johnson, Texas
- Sander M. Levin, Michigan
- Charles B. Rangel, New York

"The difference between death and taxes is death doesn't get worse every time Congress meets."

— Will Rogers
American cowboy, humorist and social commentator
1879-1935

Joint Select Committee on Deficit Reduction

Politicians got us into debt, and they have to get us out. And if the money comes from their pockets, there isn't a more appropriate source. Here are some suggestions for deficit reduction you may want to make in your letters:

- The salaries of U.S. Congress members who are worth more than $1 million dollars should be docked and donated to deficit reduction.
- Lobbying registration fees must be raised through the roof and dedicated to debt reduction.
- Raise taxes on U.S. taxpayers with the highest adjusted gross income.
- Re-route the Congress' Cost of Living Adjustment (er, annual automatic raise) to debt reduction.
- Dramatically increase taxes on U.S. corporations who manufacture outside the U.S., import foreign workers via U.S. Work Visas, and practice foreign outsourcing.
- Freeze immigration until our national debt is zero.
- Tax religious buildings, like churches, temples, mosques, rectories, basilicas. By the way, some very wise countries like Denmark, Finland and Sweden tax their churches.

- Charge a very steep annual registration fee ($1 million dollars annually) for paid corporate lobbyists.

The Joint Committee on Taxation
1625 Longworth House Office Building
Washington, DC. 20515

The Committee Members:
Patty Murray of Washington
Max Baucus of Montana
John Kerry of Massachusetts
Jon Kyl of Arizona [Up for re-election in 2012]
Rob Portman of Ohio
Patrick Toomey of Pennsylvania

"About three-quarters of registered voters (76%) say most members of Congress do not deserve re-election, the highest such percentage Gallup has measured in its 19-year history of asking this question. The 20% who say most members deserve to be re-elected is also a record low, by one percentage point." December, 2011

Read more:
http://www.care2.com/causes/vast-majority-of-americans-believe-congress-should-not-get-re-elected.html#ixzz1gqVV6n7K

12. What You and I Must Do

"If you are going through hell, keep going."
— Winston Churchill
1874-1965
Former Prime Minister of Great Britain

There's no debate about it – the 99% is going through hell.
And if we don't get moving, we'll never get out. *We have to reassert our power.* So let's move forward, shall we? Get off the couch. Buy some stamps, envelopes and start mailing your outraged letters to committee offices of U.S. Congress.

Five Things You Can Do This Week

#1. Change your voting status to "Independent." Let's scare the heck out of politicians! It'll be fun.

#2. Pull your money out of big banks. Move your holdings to your tiny local, stodgy, old-fashioned bank or credit union. After all, these small local banks follow through with meaningful, local community reinvestment initiatives.

#3. Get rid of credit and ATM Cards. These cards are the tools of thieves. The fees and arm-twisting these companies impose upon the 99% are shameful. Instead, use a Wal Mart loadable money card. There are no fees and they're just as convenient.

#4. Boycott U.S. companies who don't pay U.S. taxes. G.E., Carnival Cruises, Boeing...the list goes on and on.

#5. Read a daily newspaper. *The New York Times* or *The Wall Street Journal* are the best. Better yet, read *both*! These papers chronicle the daily activities of Congress, the political parties, lobbyists and the 1%. *You can read these papers online for free.* If you don't have web access, go online at your local library and read the papers. Read The British Times, the Financial Times, the Christian Science Monitor and The Huffington Post.

Oh and...stop wasting your time and money. Remember, the Next Big Thing is tomorrow's Old Antiquated Thing. *Is playing "Grand Theft Auto" for six hours the best use of your time?* Is *Cake Boss* really that interesting? Do you *really* need a foot-long submarine sandwich? Will the kids really *suffer* if they don't go to Orlando this spring?

Chapter 13. The Next Elections

Esquire Magazine has thoughtfully compiled a list of the worst members of 2011 Congress:

Joe Barton, Texas
Ben Nelson, Nebraska
Joe Lieberman, Connecticut
Jon Kyle, Arizona
Charlie Rangel, NY
Pete Stark, California
David Vitter, Louisiana

Don't squander your vote on another loser.
Don't be fooled by career politicians piously gazing into the camera lens, tossing around words like, "The American Family," and "reducing big government" and "our bright future." They're puppets. Ignore the politician who is still banging the drums over female reproduction, flag burning, prayer in schools or gay marriage. Those are back-burner issues *and they will forever be on the stove.* You and I both know how politicians spin these issues to avoid dealing with the *real issues.* Support only political candidates who are talking about real, actionable ways to help the 99%.

Imagine if you and I went on a job interview, and whenever we were asked a question, we brought up our religious beliefs, our feelings about gay rights and female reproduction... Do you think we'd get the job? No way!

What if voters asked really smart questions?

What if we asked politicians real questions? Enough of asking the name of their dog or their favorite song! We have to cross-examine political candidates and ask the *fundamental* questions:

- What is your plan for weaning the U.S. off of fossil fuels?
- Are you in support of Congress delivering a flexible, affordable National Health Insurance Plan for the self employed and part-time workers?
- How long would it take you to put a National Health Care plan in place?
- Would you be willing to repeal the North American Free Trade Agreement?
- Would you grant illegal immigrants amnesty?
- Would you support an immigration hiatus?
- Would you be in support of freezing all U.S. immigration until the U.S. debt is significantly reduced?
- Do you believe that health care coverage should not be attached to employment?
- Will you support the construction of a fence to seal U.S. borders?
- Would you limit election campaigning to one month?
- Are you in support of significantly raising lobbying registration fees?
- How do you plan to reduce the deficit?
- Do you think churches should pay taxes?
- How will you reform credit rating policies?
- Will you support a law requiring U.S. corporations to pay U.S. taxes?

- Will you support a bill making offshore banking and financial accounts illegal for U.S. Corporations and members of Congress?
- Do you support increasing the budget, manpower and scope of the SEC?
- Will you take a salary if your personal worth is over $1 million dollars?
- Do you support shortening the length of political campaigning to 30 days prior to Election Day?
- Do you agree that taxing Social Security and Unemployment benefits is wrong? What will you do to stop taxing Social Security and Unemployment?
- With upwards of 9% unemployment, do you agree that the U.S. shouldn't grant any work visas to non-citizens?
- Do believe that lobbying thwarts the best interests of the American people?
- How do you interact with lobbyists?
- Have you ever been a lobbyist or political consultant?
- Isn't it time that U.S. elections were held online?
- Don't you think U.S. lobbying registration fees should be raised to the million-dollar range, to help reduce the deficit?
- Members of Congress should be docked pay and benefits for compiled absences over 10%, correct?
- U.S. corporations who import non-American workers, manufacture outside of the U.S. and/or are outsourcing employment to foreign countries should pay a higher tax rate, don't you think?
- Do you support terminating all lobbying in the health care sector?
- How many hours a week will you be lobbied?
- Do you believe that paid corporate health care lobbying should be terminated?
- How do you feel about the accountability of U.S. public school teachers?

- Do you think the teacher's union should adopt merit pay?
- Although we pay the highest per-student amount in the world for public education, our students are not competitive with other countries. What's your theory for this failure?
- How much is your personal worth?
- Do you have any offshore bank accounts? Does anyone in your family have offshore bank accounts? Does your business engage in offshore banking?
- How do you feel about reducing international aid by 50% until the U.S. deficit is erased?
- Do you think the electoral college is antiquated?
- Are you behind the illegalization of High-Frequency Trading and, Robo Trading and Algorithmic Trading? (and if they don't know what it is, they're too stupid to hold office)
- During the banking crisis of 2008, was it ethical for banks --- even those defaulting banks – to continue lobbying?
- Are you ready to deploy solar, wind, electrical and renewable energy sources?
- If elected, would you accept campaign contributions from Wall Street, Big Oil or Big Pharma?
- Who has given you your biggest campaign contribution?
- Do you agree that Social Security and Medicare are off limits?
- Do you think pizza is a vegetable?

These questions will separate the puppet candidates from the candidates of substance. Hopefully, we'll start to elect members of the 99%.

Esquire's Best Members of Congress

Henry Waxman, California
Mike Pence, Indiana
Jeff Flake, Arizona
Ike Skelton, Missouri
Sheldon Whitehouse, Rhode Island
Mike Simpson, Idaho
Olympia Snowe, Maine (leaving Congress this year)

14. The New Laws We Must Fight For:

Rather than gullibly accept the empty words of professional political candidates, we must control the dialog. Overall, the smartest thing we could do is eliminate lobbying entirely. But the concepts I've listed below could spark a meaningful discourse that evolves into laws that protect the 99%.

1. Amend Section 5 of the U.S. Constitution to state that the Senate and House of Representatives are (a) not permitted to receive a Congressional paycheck if their overall gross annual earnings are over $1 million dollars (b) members of Congress are required to pay U.S. Taxes to the IRS and are prohibited from holding offshore financial accounts of any kind.

2. Absenteeism. Any member of the Senate or House of Representatives who is absent from work more than 10% will be docked that period's pay and denied benefits [unless they are near death or giving birth].

3. Political campaigns may only endure for one month (30 days) before Election Day. Britain, an older wiser country, limits their political campaigns to 4 weeks. We should too.

4. Elected officials campaigning for a new office must step down from their existing office; and will no longer receive pay or benefits.

5. Members of Congress and former members of Congress are barred from Lobby registration or grass roots lobbying and consulting.

6. Offshore bank accounts and financial holdings are illegal for employees of the U.S. government and all U.S. businesses.

7. All U.S. corporations are legally required to pay U.S. taxes.

8. U.S. corporations who grant work Visas to non-American workers, manufacture outside of the U.S. and/or are outsourcing employment to foreign countries will be subject to a higher tax rate.
9. Lobbying in the Health Care sector is hereby terminated.
10. Lobby registration fees will be raised to the million-dollar range.
11. Widen the definition of lobbying to include consulting. Limit the number of hours Congress members are permitted to be lobbied and require them to log their time/hours for the public.
12. In the event that an industry or business sector is in crisis mode, [for example, financial companies who are about to go belly-up, oil companies causing an environmental crisis] all lobbying in said sector of crisis is suspended for a 90 day period, until the crisis subsides. Violations will result in permanent loss of lobbying privileges.
13. By the end of 2012, Congress is required to offer a flexible, affordable (Monthly payment: $200 per family, $100 per individual) National Health Plan for U.S. citizens who are unemployed, self-employed or part-timers.
14. Semi-annually, U.S. public school teachers will undergo an additional dimension of evaluation determined by student critiques; Teachers' union contracts will be amended to allow termination for ineffectiveness and mediocrity.
15. The launch of a robust national initiative to replace oil, coal and gas energy sources with renewable wind, solar and electric.
16. The United States cuts international aid by 50% until our national debt is zero.
17. Build a friggin' fence protecting U.S. borders.
18. Visas are required by all foreigners visiting the U.S.

19. Freeze immigration until the national unemployment rate is reduced to 1% and the national debt is zero.
20. Make High-Frequency Trading, Robo Trading and Algorithmic Trading illegal.
21. Eliminate the electoral college.
22. Convert voting to online voting.
23. Until unemployment drops to 1%, the U.S. won't grant any work visas to non-citizens.
24. Churches and religious non-profits are required to pay taxes.
25. Social Security and Unemployment payments will no longer be taxed.
26. The SEC will quadruple in size and quadruple its efforts to investigate and prosecute financial fraud.
27. Repeal the North American Free Trade Agreement.
28. Pizza is no longer legally considered a vegetable.

Chapter 15. Complacency is Killing Us

Years ago — when we had jobs and we were able to get credit — the 99% felt okay. We felt like we were still in the game. We were going on vacations. We were able to afford Christmas. We could take our kids to a major league baseball game. Our kids were going to college. But now that we're circling the drain, we see precisely how deeply we've been pillaged by the 1%.

The 1% relies on our complacency. Politicians, the financial sector, big oil, big corporations all rely on our complacency. They rely on the fact that we're not going to read a daily newspaper. They rely on our desire for "the next big thing." The 1% mesmerizes us with "junk events" and mind-melters. But as long as a large portion of our population is completely engaged in diversions like professional sports, tattoos, gambling, piercings, the Kardashians and video games, the 1% will continue to steal us blind.

I use the word "diversion" literally – because our guilty pleasures and meaningless past-times divert our attention from the activities of the 1%. As long as they keep us addicted to mindless diversions and awaiting "the next big thing," we will never snap out of this collective trance and focus on the manipulations of the 1%.

Things the 99% can do to snap out of complacency:
1. Newspapers provide a daily account of exactly what the 1% are doing, and how they're turning every advantage for themselves. Start to read a newspaper every day.
2. Watch a <u>variety</u> of news broadcasts. Watch all of the networks, PBS *and* Fox news. Mix it up, so you can

weigh what *all* sides are selling and come to your own conclusions.

3. Reduce the number of guilty pleasures in your families' lives. The video games. The mindless cartoons. Crappy toys. Sugar-filled foods. Do we really need them? Don't buy into "the next big thing." Frankly, in our world, "the next big thing" becomes "yesterday's old thing" overnight. Blu ray, ringtones, on demand, hair extensions, Hi Def, Vios, digital, Silly Bandz, all that crap that the kids "have to have" ---- robbing us of financial security.

"The zooming wealth of the top 1 percent is a problem, but it's not nearly as big a problem as the tens of millions of Americans who have dropped out of high school or college. It's not nearly as big a problem as the 40 percent of children who are born out of wedlock. It's not nearly as big a problem as the nation's stagnant human capital, its stagnant social mobility and the disorganized social fabric for the bottom 50 percent."

— David Brooks
The New York Times
2011

Chapter 16: What the 1% are Thinking

Read the following Op Ed piece from Warren Buffet. No, not the guy who sings, *"Wasted Away Again in Margaritaville."* WARREN Buffet.

Stop Coddling the Super-Rich By WARREN E. BUFFETT

OUR leaders have asked for "shared sacrifice." But when they did the asking, they spared me. I checked with my mega-rich friends to learn what pain they were expecting. They, too, were left untouched.

While the poor and middle class fight for us in Afghanistan, and while most Americans struggle to make ends meet, we mega-rich continue to get our extraordinary tax breaks. Some of us are investment managers who earn billions from our daily labors but are allowed to classify our income as "carried interest," thereby getting a bargain 15 percent tax rate. Others own stock index futures for 10 minutes and have 60 percent of their gain taxed at 15 percent, as if they'd been long-term investors.

These and other blessings are showered upon us by legislators in Washington who feel compelled to protect us, much as if we were spotted owls or some other endangered species. It's nice to have friends in high places.

Last year my federal tax bill — the income tax I paid, as well as payroll taxes paid by me and on my behalf — was $6,938,744. That sounds like a lot of money. But what I paid was only 17.4 percent of my taxable income — and that's actually a lower percentage than was paid by any of the other 20 people in our office. Their tax burdens ranged from 33 percent to 41 percent and averaged 36 percent.

If you make money with money, as some of my super-rich friends do, your percentage may be a bit lower than mine. But if you earn money from a job, your percentage will surely exceed mine — most likely by a lot.

To understand why, you need to examine the sources of government revenue. Last year about 80 percent of these revenues came from personal income taxes and payroll taxes. The mega-rich pay income taxes at a rate of 15 percent on most of their earnings but pay practically nothing in payroll taxes. It's a different story for the middle class: typically, they fall into the 15 percent and 25 percent income tax brackets, and then are hit with heavy payroll taxes to boot.

Back in the 1980s and 1990s, tax rates for the rich were far higher, and my percentage rate was in the middle of the pack. According to a theory I sometimes hear, I should have thrown a fit and refused to invest because of the elevated tax rates on capital gains and dividends.

I didn't refuse, nor did others. I have worked with investors for 60 years and I have yet to see anyone — not even when capital gains rates were 39.9 percent in 1976-77 — shy away from a sensible investment because of the tax rate on the potential gain. People invest to make money, and potential taxes have never scared them off. And to those who argue that higher rates hurt job creation, I would note that a net of nearly 40 million jobs were added between 1980 and 2000. You know what's happened since then: lower tax rates and far lower job creation.

Since 1992, the I.R.S. has compiled data from the returns of the 400 Americans reporting the largest income. In 1992, the top 400 had aggregate taxable income of $16.9 billion and paid federal taxes of 29.2 percent on that sum. In 2008, the aggregate income of the highest 400 had soared to $90.9 billion — a staggering $227.4 million on average — but the rate paid had fallen to 21.5 percent.

The taxes I refer to here include only federal income tax, but you can be sure that any payroll tax for the 400 was inconsequential compared to income. In fact, 88 of the 400 in 2008 reported no wages at all, though every one of them reported capital gains. Some of my brethren may shun work but they all like to invest. (I can relate to that.)

I know well many of the mega-rich and, by and large, they are very decent people. They love America and appreciate the opportunity this country has given them. Many have joined the Giving Pledge, promising to give most of their wealth to philanthropy. Most wouldn't mind being told to pay more in taxes as well, particularly when so many of their fellow citizens are truly suffering.

Twelve members of Congress will soon take on the crucial job of rearranging our country's finances. They've been instructed to devise a plan that reduces the 10-year deficit by at least $1.5 trillion. It's vital, however, that they achieve far more than that. Americans are rapidly losing faith in the ability of Congress to deal with our country's fiscal problems. Only action that is immediate, real and very substantial will prevent that doubt from morphing into hopelessness. That feeling can create its own reality.

Job one for the 12 is to pare down some future promises that even a rich America can't fulfill. Big money must be saved here. The 12 should then turn to the issue of revenues. I would leave rates for 99.7 percent of taxpayers unchanged and continue the current 2-percentage-point reduction in the employee contribution to the payroll tax. This cut helps the poor and the middle class, who need every break they can get.

But for those making more than $1 million — there were 236,883 such households in 2009 — I would raise rates immediately on taxable income in excess of $1 million, including, of course, dividends and capital gains. And for those who make $10 million or more — there were 8,274 in 2009 — I would suggest an additional increase in rate.

My friends and I have been coddled long enough by a billionaire-friendly Congress. It's time for our government to get serious about shared sacrifice.

Published: August 14, 2011

— Warren E. Buffett is the chairman and chief executive of Berkshire Hathaway

Hmmm. Maybe the 1% aren't all bad. Warren Buffett seems like an honorable guy. And right now, this country is thirsting for honor.

Chapter 17. A Question of Honor

You and I thought our Congress and elected officials would do honorable things, like reform health care. We thought iconic American companies like General Electric possessed the honor to pay U.S. taxes and employ American citizens on U.S. soil. We thought the Santa Fe Chopped Salad at Friday's was far less than 1,800 calories. We've been so wrong.

The question now becomes, what has happened to American honor?

- Where is the honor in General Electric not paying U.S. taxes?
- Where is the honor in the U.S. government taxing our unemployment checks?
- Where is the honor in obstructing health care reform for American citizens?
- Where is the honor in giving billions of dollars and work to other countries?
- Was it *honorable* for the States Attorneys General to settle for a mere $25 billion from mortgage servicers guilty of foreclosure abuses, offering each wronged homeowner only up to $2,000 each?
- Where is the honor in accepting an annual paycheck of $175,000 when you're already a multi-millionaire member of Congress?
- Where is the honor in accepting government contracts and yet failing to pay U.S. taxes?
- Is it honorable for Denny's to sell the Midwestern Meat and Potatoes Sandwich when half of our population is fat?
- This list could go on and on. What would you add to this list?

The most honorable segment of the U.S. population is the members and families of the U.S. Armed Forces and National Guard. They serve at a moment's notice, travel far from their families, they aren't paid enough, and they put themselves in harm's way. They lose limbs and they die too young. *They fight wars we shouldn't have been in to begin with.* And yet they still believe in this country. That's honor. Let's protect them. Let's kick ineffective, brainless members of Congress out of Washington and replace them with thinking, caring, honorable people. And we will find honorable candidates out there — within the ranks of the 99%!

The 99% can restore American honor.
We can fill the halls of U.S. government with mail demanding change.
- We can go to town hall and change our voting status to Independent (Unenrolled). That one step alone will literally immobilize Wall Street and Washington.
- We can read a newspaper every day.
- We can ask serious questions of our politicians before we vote for them. We can demand proof that they know how to get things done on behalf of the 99%.
- We can hold Congress accountable and not re-elect members who haven't accomplished anything for us.
- We can change the structure of U.S. political campaigning, reduce campaign durations and prevent members of the 1% from controlling the game.
- We can reduce and eliminate Washington lobbyists.
- We can stop being doormats. We can realize the power in numbers that we wield, and use it! We are --- after all – the 99%.

You can fully expect people to renounce these proposals. I am prepared for people to call these ideas crazy, blasphemous, socialist, communist and maybe even radical. If members of Congress can convince a nation that pizza is a vegetable, comparatively, my suggestions look tame. And so what if these proposals are "outside of the box"? Remember, America was founded by radicals. And last I checked, this is still the home of the brave.

The 1% fully expect you to not read this book. The powerbrokers rely upon you to remain on the couch, eating a roll of raw cookie dough and watching a Scooby Doo marathon. They want you to get into fistfights over who should have won "Dancing With The Stars." They are counting on you to worry about the Kardashians, run off to a bar, pound beers and end the evening in a tattoo parlor. They hope and pray you get your news from *Entertainment Tonight*. They like the fact that you believe Elvis Presley is still alive. And they assume you're not going to help fix what's wrong with America.

Prove them wrong.

"If we all did the things we are capable of, we would astound ourselves."

— Thomas Edison
Inventor
1847-1931

THE END
(hopefully it's a new beginning)

About the Author

My name is not on this book because the insights and ideas within this manifesto are more important than personal recognition.

The dishonorable behavior of our politicians, paid corporate lobbyists, American corporations and Wall Street must end. We've all worked too hard to be treated so shabbily by the people we put in power. And yet, they get away with their misdeeds because we're not keeping an eye on them.

Let's not allow the 1% to dishonor us any more.

Let's repair our financial standings and restore honor to this country by paying attention to what the 1% is doing. Let's stop them from doing things that aren't in the best interests of the 99%.

We will triumph because there's strength in numbers, and we are the 99%.

Anonymously Yours,
Me